Magical
World
Coloring Book

Magical
World
Coloring Book

Enchanting images to
spirit you away

SIRIUS

SIRIUS

This edition published in 2022 by Sirius Publishing, a division of
Arcturus Publishing Limited,
26/27 Bickels Yard, 151–153 Bermondsey Street,
London SE1 3HA

Copyright © Arcturus Holdings Limited

ISBN: 978-1-3988-2247-4
CH007277NT
supplier 29, Date 0622, Print run PI00002223

Printed in China

Introduction

Steal away to a magical world filled with elfin figures, fairytale castles, decorative landscapes, and psychedelic abstracts. These imaginative scenes for coloring will impart a sense of wonder, not just with the world of fantasy but with the magic that is all around us.

The beauty of coloring is that each person can bring his or her own interpretation to the image in front of them. You can choose to color the page any way you like, with soft, subtle hues or vibrant neon shades, so that the artwork you produce is completely your own.

So grab a set of colored pens or pencils – your magical mystery tour starts here!

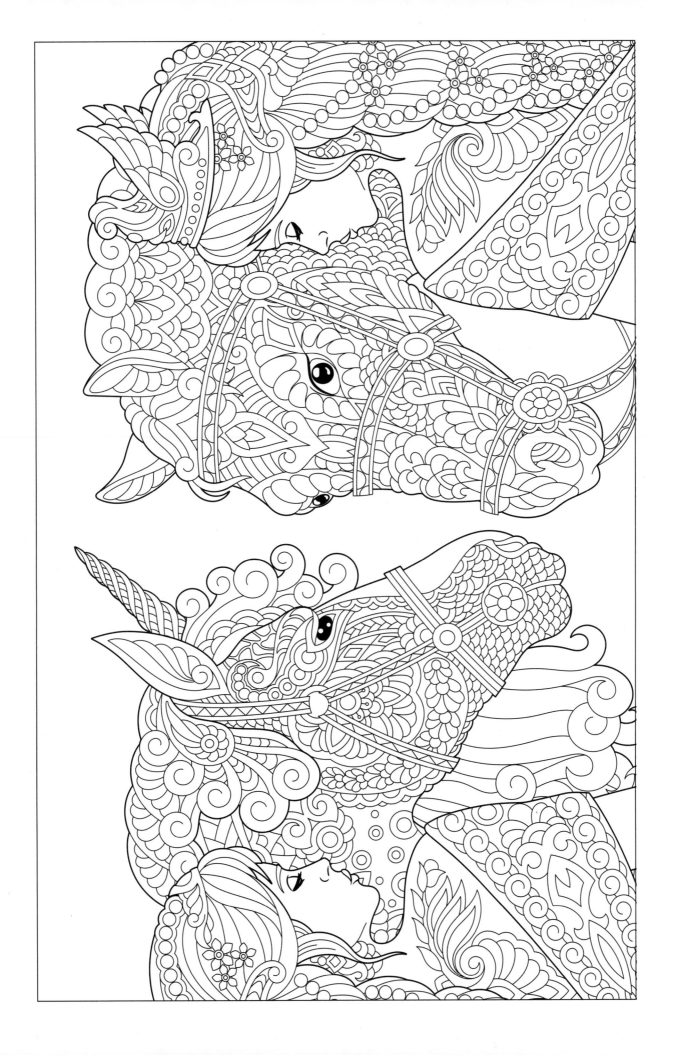

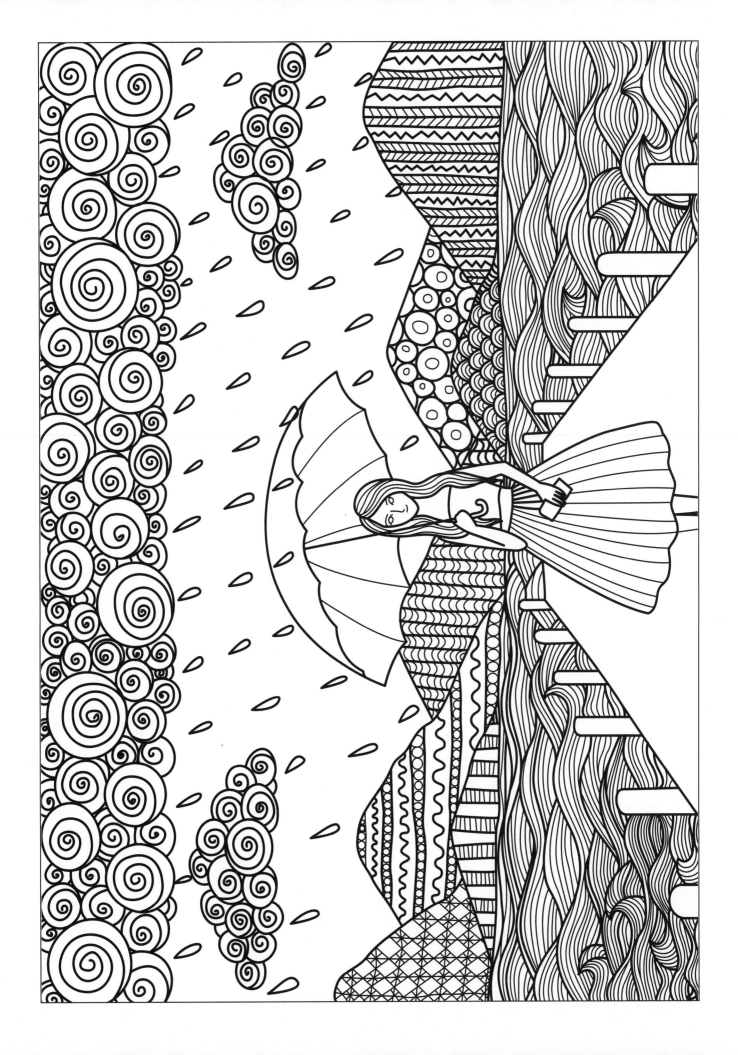